THE
MOON
OF
FALLING LEAVES

THE
MOON
OF
FALLING
LEAVES

The Great Buffalo Hunt

BY CARY B. ZITER
ILLUSTRATED BY GRETCHEN WILL MAYO

FRANKLIN WATTS
New York/London/Toronto/Sydney/1988

Library of Congress Cataloging-in-Publication Data

Ziter, Cary B.
The moon of falling leaves : the great buffalo hunt / by Cary
B. Ziter; illustrated by Gretchen Will Mayo.
p.   cm.
Bibliography: P.
Includes index.
Summary: Depicts the central importance of the buffalo in the life
of the Plains Indians by tracing a year in the cycle of hunting,
herding, and deriving products and food from the buffalo.
ISBN 0-531-10502-4
1. Indians of North America—Great Plains—Hunting—Juvenile
literature. 2. Indians of North America—Great Plains—Social life
and customs—Juvenile literature. 3. Bison, American—Juvenile
literature. [1. Indians of North America—Great Plains—Hunting.
2. Indians of North America—Great Plains—Social life and customs.
3. Bison.] I. Mayo, Gretchen, ill. II. Title.
E78.G73Z57   1988
978'.00497—dc19   87-25164 CIP AC

CONTENTS

For Joanne, Jesse, and Claire

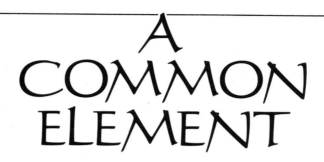

A COMMON ELEMENT

The Great Plains of North America was a land once ruled by millions of bison. For many centuries, these animals wandered aimlessly across the continent, pawing at the grass here, wallowing in the mud there, walking off for a drink of cold water in a racing river.

In this huge, middle section of the United States, there were deer and many birds; there were rabbits, snakes, wolves, and prairie dogs; there were dozens of animals to be used for food, clothing, or both. But mostly there were the buffalo, great shaggy beasts in herds so large they blackened the entire horizon. In every direction they fed, in nearly every corner of this beautiful land they grazed and marched with solemn dignity.

Buffalo roamed in four great herds over the American prairie: the Texas herd, Arkansas herd, Republican herd, and Northern herd, which overlapped each other because the herds moved with the seasons. No one knows exactly how many of these animals ran with the wind on the Great Plains. One estimate puts the number of buffalo alive there in the early and middle 1800s at 40 million, while another puts it at a staggering 100 million: 60 to 75 million animals is the number given most often. Several soldiers on a trip to Kansas, for example, recalled seeing perhaps 4 million buffalo in a massive swarm 50 miles (80 km) deep and 25 miles (40 km) wide—and that was but one of many herds!

These great hairy mammals were an essential element in the life of the American Indians of the Great Plains, major tribes such as the Crow, Assiniboin, Blackfoot, Cheyenne, Sioux, Pawnee, and Kiowa, to name but a few. The various ways by which these people hunted and used buffalo offer a fascinating view of how the Indians lived and worked.

The West of yesterday was a place of many tribes speaking various languages and following different ways of life. Trading habits, forms of government, family life, style of warfare, funeral customs, and art differed greatly from tribe to tribe. The various Great Plains cultures, too, were a mixture of wandering hunters and village farmers. The Mandans, for example, were a tribe of the Upper Missouri that was well off early in its history thanks to successful farming—and it always clung to that tradition. The Cheyenne, however, by the mid-1800s, had entirely replaced their farm economy with buffalo hunting. Both tribes, as well as all the other Great Plains tribes, hunted buffalo at some time in the year in one way or another.

Left: *Cheyenne woman, Sioux dressed for buffalo hunt,
and a Mandan in buffalo robe and headdress*
Above: *buffalo emerging from lower earth*

As with other cultural customs, each tribe had its own story-telling tradition. There are many tales associated with the birth of the buffalo, though several echo the theme found in this tale of creation told by the Sioux:

In the days of the grandfathers, buffalo lived under the earth. In the olden times, they say, a man who was journeying came to a hill where many holes in the ground were. He entered one of them. When he had gone inside he found buffalo chips and buffalo tracks on all sides. He found also buffalo hair where the buffalo had rubbed against the walls. These were the real buffalo, and they lived under the ground. Afterward, some of them came to the surface of the earth and lived there. Then the herds on the earth increased.[1]

THE
HORSE

When the buffalo once living "under the earth" began roaming the high, swaying prairie grass of middle America, Indian tribes living on this bountiful land began following the great herds. This was possible, of course, only after they acquired the horse. The coming of the horse made moving about easy, and many tribes began to travel widely. By the 1700s, the use of the horse for buffalo hunting was probably widespread. If the food supply moved, the Indians could move with it. People who had sometimes been haunted by starvation in the past now were food-rich and satisfied most of the time.

Horses had been brought to North America by Spaniards in the 1500s. As soon as Great Plains tribes discovered the animals, they became intoxicated by their speed, power, grace, and usefulness in war and hunting. Their cultures were forever changed. The men of tribes such as the Comanches were atop an unshod pony from boyhood to old age, the horse their welcome and constant companion.

Galloping across the ridges, prairies, and hills, the Indians must have felt as if they had discovered the power of thunder and the speed of lightning. They became one with the land on these magnificent animals. With the horse, the hunt became more frequent and the number of animals killed increased. As the Blackfoot Many-Tail-Feathers noted, "Tribes frequently moved camp." To put it another way, they became more "nomadic."

Personal wealth was measured by the number of fine mounts an Indian owned. Wolf Calf, a warrior in the Piegan band of the Blackfoot tribe, recalled the story of the tribe's first sight of horses.[1] He said the Piegans were hunting on foot when one day enemy warriors of the Kutenai appeared on horseback. The Piegans were astonished and afraid and stared in disbelief. Did these four-legged, long-maned creatures come from the sun, or did

*Piegans seeing horses
for the first time*

they come out of the earth as the buffalo did? The Piegan chief was terrified as the Kutenai trotted forward. The Kutenai chief made a sign that he was friendly and patted his horse on the neck.

"I give you this animal," he said.

The Piegans and Kutenai became friends, with the Kutenai eventually bringing many horses to the Piegans' camp for them to see.

"When they first got horses," Wolf Calf recalled, "the people did not know what they fed on. They would offer the animals pieces of fat and rub their noses with it, to try to get them to eat it. Then the horses would turn away and put down their heads and begin to eat the grass of the prairie."

The buffalo were also nomadic, roaming in the course of a year over vast areas of the country, searching for food and water. These migrations were toward the south in the winter, where warmer weather prevailed, then back north again in the spring. It wasn't uncommon for a herd to move 400 miles (650 km). When the buffalo moved in large bands across the plains, their path was marked sometimes by the column of dust they raised.

Given the diversity of their cultures, hunting habits and times of the hunt varied from tribe to tribe. With many American Indians, however, large, well-organized buffalo hunts involving the entire tribe were held twice a year, first in the spring, then in the fall. For the Sioux, the autumn hunt took place in October, a month they called the Moon of Falling Leaves, a time when the buffalo put on winter fat and grew a thick, dark-brown fur that made splendid robes.

BUFFALO DANCE

Many tribes wouldn't start the seasonal communal hunt until a ceremony was held—a buffalo dance asking the heavenly spirits for aid in finding large herds. Tribal leaders or medicine men would dance to the sound of rattles and drums in a ceremony often quite loud. The Mandans, for example, held their dance in the center of the village, an area roughly resembling a public square. In front of the tribe's medicine lodge, ten or fifteen Mandans danced joyously, each wearing a buffalo mask with horns on it and shaking a favorite bow or lance. With drums pounding and rattles shaking, the warriors yelled incessantly as onlookers nervously waited their turn to jump into the ring of dancers, all of whom moved about until fatigue overcame them. Such ceremonies sometimes lasted several days until the joyful moment when scouts brought the word to camp that the much needed buffalo herds finally had appeared.

Comanches placed buffalo skulls on the prairie with the horns and "eyes" facing camp to encourage the Great Spirit to send the herd in their direction. Blackfoot used the *iniskim* (buffalo stone) in a mystic ceremony. This marine shell was thought to have the magical power to attract buffalo. Cheyenne wore the *issiwun*, a sacred cap made of buffalo hide with two hand-painted buffalo horns attached. The Sioux believed the eagle would bring a message to the tribe announcing the arrival of the buffalo, and they would sing this song:

He! They have come back racing,
He! They have come back racing,
Why, they say there is to be a buffalo hunt over here.
Make arrows! Make arrows!
Says the father, says the father.
Give me my knife,
Give me my knife,
I shall hang up the meat to dry—Ye' ye!
I shall hang up the meat to dry—Ye' ye!
Says grandmother—Yo' yo!
Says grandmother—Yo' yo![1]

SCOUTS AND POLICE

Plains Indian tribes carried out the communal buffalo hunts under the watchful eyes of tribal police. They also used scouts to help locate the roving herds.

Going out to scout for buffalo was known as "going to the hills." Life in camp could be anxious as everyone waited for the scouts to return. One good account of the scouts' activity was written by Thomas Lawrence Riggs, who accompanied a tribe of Sioux hunters in 1880.[1] It is common to find accounts of American Indian activity recorded by people who pushed into the West. Indians have a rich and varied history, but they didn't keep records as we know them, so many of their stories come to us from the frontiersmen, missionaries, traders, or scholars who spent time among them.

"It was just before sunset that our runners came into view and the entire camp went wild,"[2] Riggs recalled.

Carrying word that they had spotted a herd, the scouts came straight to an older man who was designated crier, or camp herald. The elder would light a pipe, take a whiff of smoke, then touch the earth with the pipe before lifting it skyward.

"You have grown up among these hills and valleys. Tell me, I pray, if you have seen anything of prowling wolf or flying buzzard or feeding animal beyond the hills whence you come; tell me truly and make me glad,"[3] the elder said to one of the scouts.

Sioux scouts returning to camp

Old man with pipe honoring scouts' return

The scout received the pipe and took a mouthful of smoke, in turn offering it to earth and sky, then passing the pipe to his fellow runners. He answered that he had indeed seen buffalo. The other men then cried a shrill and joyful, "Hai-ee! Hai-ee!"

"We shall have plenty of meat by this time tomorrow,"[4] said the elder.

With the herds in sight, it was time for the actual hunt, always a group activity demanding success: a good kill insured an adequate supply of meat for the winter. For this reason, the hunters were policed by a group of their peers. The expedition involved the entire village marching toward the herd with the order of an army. The tribal police imposed a strict rule of silence once the animals were actually in sight, for even the slightest noise might frighten the buffalo. People who broke the rules received severe punishment.

Consider the case of two Cheyenne hunters.[5] Everyone had been given specific orders by police that they were not to hunt alone. Temptation, however, was too strong for both sons of Two Forks, who were caught shooting at the herd before the signal was given. Little Old Man, in charge of the hunting party, fumed when he learned of this. He ordered loyal hunters to whip the violators.

"Those who fail or hesitate shall get a beating themselves,"[6] Little Old Man shouted.

Horses charged into the valley where the two men hunted. The two violators must have looked up in dismay. Instantly, their horses were shot out from under them, their guns were smashed, and they were slashed with riding whips by each of their fellow hunters.

Such was the punishment administered by tribal police to those who broke the rules.

CHASE, SURROUND

Methods of hunting the buffalo among American Indians varied at different times and at different locations. As with all other aspects of daily life, the hunts were carried out in accordance with the customs of the various tribes that called the expansive Great Plains their home.

After the coming of the horse, the most common hunting methods were the chase and the surround. Prior to the horse, and occasionally after its introduction, the impound and the jump were used. Before and after the horse, a method of killing buffalo called the still hunt was employed.

The chase certainly was the most exciting method of buffalo hunting—and the most dangerous.

When the scouts had done their work, and the hunters were near the herd, the group leader dispatched the men to their designated positions. Every step was cautious, for any sudden movement, something as simple as the bark of a prairie dog or a passing shadow, might stampede the buffalo herd assembled in the valley below the armed horsemen. The moment before the charge was tense: young men and old warriors alike shook with excitement. Finally, the leader let out a sharp cry and the army swooped down on the unsuspecting animals.

Sioux horsemen waiting in rocks above the buffalo

Buffalo spread out in small bands over large areas while grazing. When excited and on the run, however, they formed a tightly packed mass. Suddenly, the plain was a sea of darkened bodies thundering across the rolling hills, plowing through the high grass like a knife through butter. Dust, thick and nasty, clouded the air. The grunts of the frightened beasts echoed for miles. The earth trembled. The bold horsemen picked out a heaving, grunting target. Bows often were used, even after the hunters traded with pioneers for rifles. The bow was made of a wood called Osage orange or of horn wrapped with twisted sinews of deer for extra strength. The bow was only 3 feet (about 1 m) long, making the weapon easy to handle atop the fleetest pony. Each hunter identified his own arrow through markings on the shaft or by the feathers at the end. A well-trained hunter could shoot these missiles with incredible speed and accuracy.

The horses, trained for the task, darted in and out among the chocolate-brown animals at the simplest command, often reacting to the slightest pressure from the knees of the rider. The Indian drew a few arrows from his quiver and selected a fat bull on the outskirts of the herd. The horses separated the animal from the rest of the herd. The hunter tried to shoot between the protruding hip bone and the last rib of the animal, with the arrow zipping forward into the heart or, better, the lungs. His bow was accurate between 30 and 50 yards (27 and 46 m). A hunter who placed too many arrows into a raging bull would be teased later by the women of the tribe.

Dangers in the chase were many. The horns of the buffalo were so sharp that a quick swish of the head of a terrified prey could easily slash a horse's stomach wide open. Or a horse could trip in a prairie-dog hole and send its master tumbling to earth, where he might be gored or trampled to death by the blindly fleeing bulls. Sometimes a hunter used a long, sharp lance instead of a bow and arrow. It took more strength and daring to hunt this way, so the man who did this successfully was showered with compliments.

*Horsemen pulling
arrows from bull*

Wounded buffalo

A grand rush by hunters with six-shooters and rifles instead of more primitive weapons came late in the Great Plains Indians' hunting history. The actual chase with advanced weapons, however, followed the same procedure of dashing into the herd to single out a buffalo on the edge of the group for the kill, then repeating the process as many times as possible until the herd had run too far away for the hunters to pursue.

How frightful the bulls must have looked: their dangling goat-like beards wet with saliva, their tongues hanging out, their eyes bloodshot, blazing, maddened with pain. Their gallop seemed clumsy, but they were fast-moving creatures. Wroo-wroo-wroo! The sound of the wounded bulls echoed across the untamed plains until finally the fur-covered creatures dropped in the shadow of the mounted antagonists. The hunters rode in clouds of dust, in the company of dozens of other horsemen, crossing and recrossing each other's tracks. They rode among dead, wounded, or terrified, fleeing animals. But despite an hour of such wild, bewildering confusion, the hunter usually was able to find the spot where the animal he killed had fallen and identify it as his own.

The surround was dangerous too. It was similar to the chase, though it could be accomplished on foot as well as on horseback. The purpose was simple enough: to form a ring around a few animals and tighten it little by little until the hunters were close

The surround

The surround

enough to destroy them. Here, too, mounted warriors were often chased by angry buffalo and they had to use all their great skill as horsemen to wheel their mounts and quickly escape. Eventually, though, they would turn on the beasts again. Sometimes a hunter would snatch a buffalo robe from his waist and throw it over the eyes and horns of the prey. This confused the animal and allowed the men to kill it. The surround method was effective, for it is said that in 1830 a group of Sioux hunters killed 1,500 buffalo in a single surround.

STILL HUNT

Unlike the chase, the still hunt wasn't a tribal affair. Instead, much smaller groups of hunters would go "downwind" of the buffalo: that is, with the wind blowing away from the herd toward the hunters. They did this so the buffalo could not pick up their scent, for the nose of the buffalo was keen. Although the prairie grass swayed as the men moved, and there was little else for cover, the hunters often went undetected. Part of this may be attributed to a clever disguise. Buffalo were used to seeing packs of wolves. Wherever the buffalo went, the scavengers followed, waiting to prey on an undefended calf, a wounded cow, or an old grumpy bull straying from the herd in search of solitude. Indians would kill a wolf, skin it, and wear the fur as they crawled on all fours toward a buffalo singled out for the kill. With one animal down, the Indian would hide behind it and kill other animals before the herd smelled blood and was aware of the danger.

❮ IMPOUNDING ❯

Impounding also was less dangerous than the chase, though certainly more active for the tribe than the still hunt. Some scholars doubt the accuracy of reports on this method given the prairie's lack of raw building materials and the buffalo's ability to smash man-made pens. Still, accounts of impounding can be found. Northern Plains Indians, for example, were said to impound buffalo by driving them into a man-made corral. This took a great deal of preparation since the corral was constructed of stone, timber, and piled brush. One such enclosure was 125 feet (38 m) in diameter. Rows of bushes forming winged V-like fences extended out from the structure and served to guide buffalo into the pen. These long rows, called the "dead men" by some tribes, were made of stone if wood was not available. The bleached bones of dead buffalo sometimes were used too.

Hunters stationed themselves behind these barricades as other tribesmen drove the animals toward them. If a raging buffalo tried to jump the fence, a man quickly popped up and waved a buffalo robe to urge the angered beast onward. Once inside the corral, the buffalo rushed about wildly. Screaming to scare the animals, the hunters climbed atop the wooden corral and began slaughtering the bewildered creatures. (Anyone who slipped off the fence was usually seriously injured or killed.)

*A diagram showing impounding—Northern Plains Indians
making a corral of stone, timber, and piled brush*

*Young boy in buffalo disguise leading
buffalo to mouth of corral*

Sometimes this method went sour. A frantic old bull might see a narrow crevice in the corral not closed by bushes or wooden fence. If so, he dashed for it and smashed through. As was their custom, the entire herd followed the leader. Running helter-skelter after the animal leader, many buffalo might manage to escape in the panic without injury.

Blackfeet and Assiniboin Indians impounded with the help of a swift member of the tribe who made believe he was a buffalo. The youth started toward a band of buffalo at daylight. He carried a shaggy hide and buffalo head as a disguise. Nearing the herd, wearing his animal costume, he knelt in the grass and bleated like a buffalo calf. Then he made his way toward the mouth of the fence leading into the trap. He repeated the cry until the curious buffalo eventually followed the decoy. At the same time, mounted warriors rode at the rear of the herd urging it forward. A crowd of women and children also ran along screaming, adding to the animals' confusion. As the buffalo were shoved closer to the corral, their behavior grew more frantic. They bellowed, kicked, and jumped wildly. Once they were inside the enclosure, however, the slaughter was simple, quick, and with little risk to the hunters.

THE JUMP

Clever disguises also played a part in the buffalo jump, in which the animals were killed by running them off a cliff. Tribes that employed this method called on a young man to fasten a buffalo robe to his body and place a buffalo hat, horns and all, on his head. Then they sought out a band of buffalo milling close to a high cliff or river running through certain areas of Montana or the Dakotas. Covered with the robe, the lone hunter eased into sight of the herd, though never straying too far from the bank of the waterway. Mounted companions then rushed the herd from the opposite direction. Small groups of buffalo quickly united in a dark mass of power resembling a speeding locomotive. The alarmed herd raced off. The leading buffalo, however, spotted what it thought was a lone animal in the distance. The leader of the crazed group ran toward the disguised Indian, apparently thinking it was a fellow buffalo that had discovered safety.

With the herd but a few hundred feet away, the decoy sped toward the cliff at full speed. He quickly located a deep crevice that he had sought out prior to the hunt and crawled into it for protection. The racing buffalo didn't realize what was happening. Suddenly, it was too late for the one-ton beasts to change direction. Those in front of the raging herd tumbled headlong over the

The jump

cliff or jump. The hunters then simply rode or walked down the riverbank and picked the choicest meat. One early nineteenth century account says 700 buffalo were killed at one time this way.

Crow Indians were known to use the jump, which was ideally suited to the rugged, jagged areas of Montana and northern Wyoming they called home. There is a Crow legend associated with this technique. Joseph Medicine Crow said it was Old Man Coyote, a figure in the Crow's mythology, who gave the Crow the idea of forcing buffalo over cliffs.

Old Man Coyote was hungry one day and so were the rest of the people, and he decided to go look for some meat. Soon he found a herd of buffalo. . . . He decided to trick them over a nearby cliff hidden by a thick cloud of fog. In his usual bragging style, he challenged the head buffalo to a race. Well, as the story goes, his challenge was immediately accepted and the race was on. Naturally Old Man Coyote selected the course, was ahead, and when they approached the cliff, he disappeared quickly. The buffalo herd went over the cliff.[1]

WINTER

Winter was not a time for well-planned hunts as was the Moon of Falling Leaves or the spring hunting season. When white blankets of dancing snowflakes covered the land like diamonds, the Great Plains tribes made permanent camp and no longer followed the buffalo. Small family parties continued to leave camp if necessary, but for the most part the ponies were too weak and thin to travel long distances in the cold. Piles of packed snow also made it impossible for the horses to run. Warriors stayed inside warm tepees, making bows and arrows and other needed tools, or telling stories of great hunts and glorious victories in war.

Buffalo, of course, were not completely safe in the winter. They bogged down in the snow, unable to move rapidly. A single warrior often could simply walk up to the animal and kill it with little or no trouble.

While camping between the junction of the Little Big Horn and Big Horn rivers in what is now Montana, Two Leggings, a Crow warrior, was asked by Pretty Face, another Crow, to go hunting.[1] Two Leggings, a minor leader of his tribe born around 1847, saw that his people needed food, and despite the harshness of Old Man Winter, he accepted the hunting challenge. Pretty Face's wife went along to drive the spare horses. The horses moved slowly as they left camp. Two Leggings soon pulled away from the others, having decided to search for a bull on his own.

A Great Plains tribe's permanent camp for winter

Buffalo trapped in snow

Two Leggings and bull watching

He climbed a bluff and looked down on the Big Horn Valley. He quickly spotted a small band of buffalo nosing the snow for grass. The wind, blowing his way, allowed him to move in close. Two Leggings singled out a fat two-year-old bull and shot it with a rifle. The snow, however, was not deep enough to keep the animal from running. Although it fell several times, it kept getting to its feet. Finally, it stumbled one last time and collapsed beside a tree.

Two Leggings approached the animal. Its tail moved, and, suddenly, it charged. Two Leggings squeezed off another bullet, but it was a wild shot. He threw the gun down and ran, but crashed into the bank of a little hollow and fell on his back. The bull swerved past him, ran up a little hill, and stood silently for a moment, staring at the Crow and shaking its head. Red froth dripped from its mouth and its eyes were bloodshot. Still, it would not fall. Whenever Two Leggings tried to roll over, the buffalo pawed the ground angrily as if ready to charge again. The hunter's blanket had slipped off his shoulder when he fell, but each time he reached for it, the buffalo stepped closer.

A long time passed. Two Leggings prayed to the Great Above Person for help. Suddenly, he heard voices—Pretty Face was atop the river bluff overlooking him, sadly telling his wife that Two Leggings must be dead. At that moment, the bull charged. Two Leggings screamed. Instantly, Pretty Face tossed his friend a rope. Two Leggings grabbed it and scrambled to safety.

"Pretty Face told the bull that it had almost killed his friend, then put an arrow through its heart,"[2] Two Leggings said.

Building a fire to get warm, the trio was soon eating and laughing about Two Leggings running into the bank.

"That night I dreamt buffalo were standing all around me, pawing the ground and making the snow fly. I was on my back growing very cold. When I woke up, my robe had fallen off and I was shivering."[3]

FOOD, CLOTHING

What did buffalo-hunting tribes do with the animals they killed by the chase, the surround, still hunting, impounding, or the jump?

The Spanish explorers of the Southwest, and other Europeans who later pushed into the heartland of America, marveled at the vast herds of buffalo which they encountered. They quickly learned from natives that the buffalo, as one Assiniboin tribesman put it, "was more than an animal. It was the staff of life. No other animal gave so much to the people as the great shaggy creature."[1]

This admired animal—bison is the buffalo's scientific name—was not a commodity to be wasted foolishly by the Indians. This truth, however, needs just a bit of qualification.

The popular idea held by many readers of the history of the American West might be that only the invading white hunters and traders pushing onto the Great Plains from the original thirteen colonies wasted buffalo, soiled the land, or polluted the water. Several scholarly studies show that this is not the case. It is known, for example, that a variety of furs and skins were traded by Indians to white mountainmen in the 1830s, but at this early date, the emphasis was clearly on the buffalo robe. Indians increased their production of choice winter robes to meet the new demand since summer robes were too thin: *teshna'ha* said the Omaha, meaning "hide without hair." The market for buffalo robes grew from

Indians trading buffalo skin

approximately 25,000 robes a year in the early 1830s to at least 90,000 robes a year by 1840. By 1854 the number had increased to 150,000 robes annually.[2] There is another example, too, of a large band of 500 to 600 Sioux Indians in 1833 killing 1,400 buffalo in South Dakota and taking only the tongues, considered a great delicacy. When such methods as the jump were used for hunting, there was no way to control the number of animals killed, sometimes causing many dead buffalo to be left behind, rotting, wasted, and little more than free food for the wolves.

Despite such examples, though, historians agree the buffalo was not in danger of extermination even as late as the middle 1800s. The number of white hunters at this time was still relatively small given the number of buffalo. Additionally, natural predators such as wolves and bears, disease, winter storms, and even the Indians' taking of thousands of buffalo year after year made but a small dent in the huge herds. Nature took its course: every year the bulls and cows mated, every year the herds replenished enough to keep them awesome and well spread across the whole of the Great Plains.

To the Indians the land was a place to be adored, a place where they could run with no fences or buildings or train tracks to stop them; a place to ride a horse at the speed of lightning; a place of solitude where in a dream one could hear the thundering of distant hooves. How could they not adore a land where the sky wore a shirt of iron blue, where the water was clear, and where the grass waved freely as if a thousand farm girls were holding straw hats to the wind.

Perhaps Chief Luther Standing Bear best expressed the collective attitude of the many tribes regarding their feelings toward the land:

We are of the soil and the soil is of us. We love the birds and beasts that grew with us on this soil. They drank the same water we did and breathed the same air. We are all one in nature. Believing so, there was in our hearts a great peace and a welling kindness for all living, growing things.[3]

*Even wolves killing buffalo made but a small
dent in the population of the herds.*

There was some waste and excessive killing at times, but for the
most part natives of the North American continent were incredibly creative in their use of the buffalo. Almost every part of the
animal became food, clothing, tools, shelter, or decorative ornaments used in tribal ceremonies.

Making all these things was a lot of work, with the process
starting as soon as the hunters finished killing the animals. The
women did the heavy work of butchering and skinning.

Dressing twenty-five to thirty robes was "considered an
excellent winter's work for one woman,"[4] though the average was
about eighteen to twenty each. The dead buffalo were set upon
immediately after the kill. Each animal belonged to the man who

Women dressing hides

killed it, although he was expected to share with the needy. The hunter easily identified his property by looking at the marked arrows in the hide. The animals were disemboweled, the various chunks of meat cut up and bagged in hides, then loaded aboard pack horses for hauling back to camp. Plains tribes were sharing tribes, so the elders made sure everyone got a portion of the kill. No one went hungry when there was food.

Sometimes women, children, and the hunters took time for buffalo delicacies right on the spot, drinking warm blood, eating raw brains, or sucking marrow from the center of freshly cracked bones. On the days to follow, when fresh meat was eaten, it would be cooked on pointed sticks over the fire, or more often than not, boiled in water, apparently the most popular way to prepare food. Comanches left the buffalo's heart when butchering the animal. This, they believed, allowed the buffalo's spirit to live and thus replenish the world with an abundance of the shaggy masters of the Great Plains.

Dressing the hides was a tedious task demanding skill and patience. The women of the tribe would first remove flesh and gristle by staking out hides and scraping them with a chisel-like tool made from buffalo or elk bone. The hide then was allowed to dry before being scraped again. If the skin was not to be used as a robe, it was turned over so the hair could be removed with a scraper. At this point, the hide was as stiff as a board. It had to be soaked in water, eventually getting pliable enough for final treatment with a mixture of brains, liver, and fats. Women prepared this paste by squeezing the ingredients with their hands, then spreading it over the skins. Finally, the skin was rubbed repeatedly over twisted rawhide thongs to completely break down the tissue to a soft texture.

Hides were used for tepees, clothing, moccasins, drums, braided ropes, carrying bags, or shields in battle. Summer and winter hides had different uses. Hides not scraped of hair became robes for sleeping and wearing during the winter. Even buffalo hair was useful. Braided, it became a bracelet or wiglike ornament worn in religious ceremonies; spun or woven, it became a blanket; in the winter, it was stuffed in moccasins to help keep feet warm. Bones were used for digging, jewelry, or bows; horns for

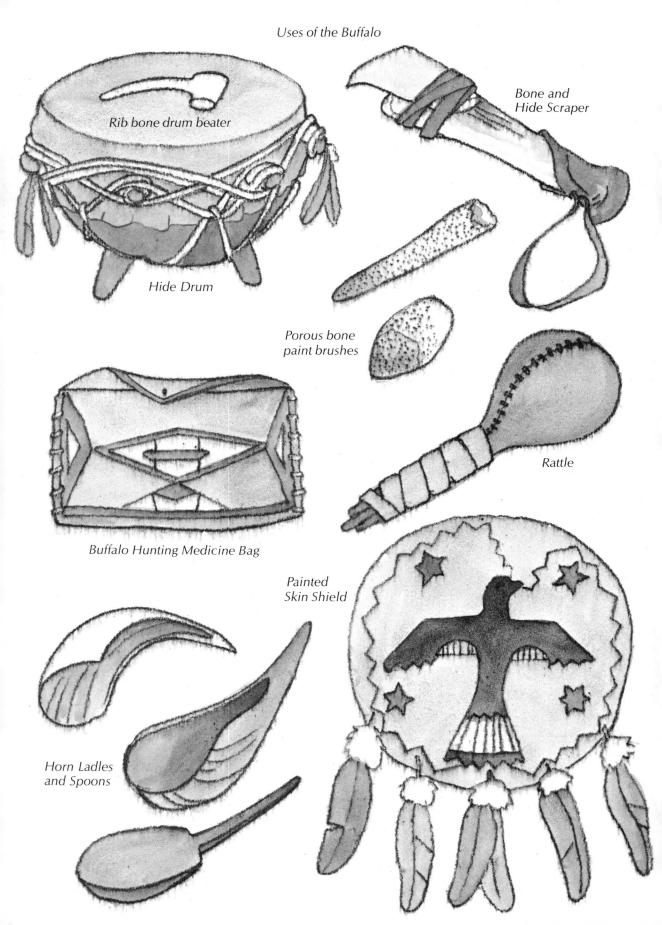

Uses of the Buffalo

Rib bone drum beater

Hide Drum

Bone and Hide Scraper

Porous bone paint brushes

Buffalo Hunting Medicine Bag

Rattle

Painted Skin Shield

Horn Ladles and Spoons

Uses of the Buffalo

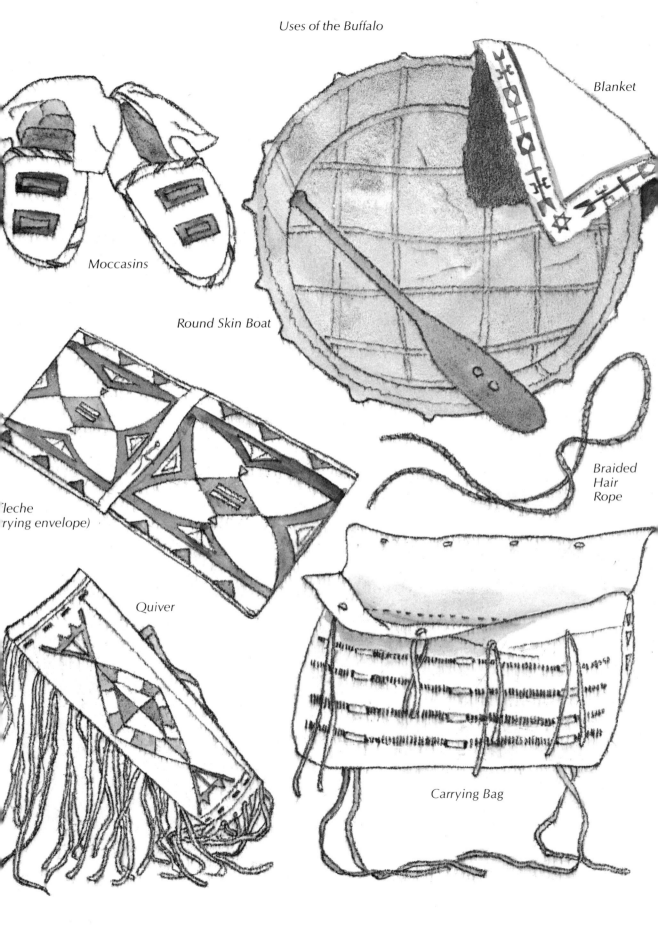

Moccasins

Blanket

Round Skin Boat

Braided
Hair
Rope

Parfleche
(carrying envelope)

Quiver

Carrying Bag

Drying jerky

drinking. Hooves boiled down made a glue used to fasten feathers on arrows. Sinew furnished bowstrings, threads for sewing, and fiber for ropes.

Since some tribes traveled great distances, they devised a way to keep meat for long periods. Much of it was "jerked," that is, cut into strips about a quarter-inch (0.6cm) thick and allowed to dry thoroughly. Women simply hung the strips from a wooden rack to swing in the breeze like a shirt on a clothesline. Some of these strips, packed in hide sacks and transported on horseback, were made into pemmican.

Pemmican was an important food source for the Plains tribes—it was highly nutritious and portable, and it kept well for a long time. To make it, the women placed the buffalo meat in boiling water and then added hot tallow and berries or herbs. This concoction was poured into little cakes and became rock-hard when cool. A winter's supply for many families could be hidden in a hole lined with buffalo hides. Such a cache saved many lives in the harsh winter months when fresh meat couldn't be found. When it was time to eat it, the pemmican was thrown into boiling water and soon became a soft, tasty, protein-rich meal.

THE HUNTING ENDS

So it was that for an untold number of years, many Indian tribes of the Great Plains hunted the huge sea of buffalo in the region between the Mississippi River and the Rocky Mountains, and from northern Texas all the way to the Canadian border of Montana and the Dakotas. Indian hunters were at the height of their glory chasing the creatures through the prairie grass. At times, the hunt was thin, the land cold, desolate, and barren. Yet the Indians did not wish to change their life. It was only the coming of huge numbers of invading pioneers and the railroads that made them do so.

Pretty Shield, a Crow from Montana, remembered the first time she saw the strangely dressed, hairy-faced "white" people. She was only "six snows old." They were trappers traveling in a canoe on the upper Missouri River. This is why at first the Crow called the white men *Beta-awk-a-wha-cha,* which means "Sits on the water."

"My mother told me that these white men had asked if they might stay with our people, and that Walks With The Moon had answered no, giving them a night and a day to rest before going away."[1]

Just a few decades after many Indians first saw the white man, their tribes saw something even stranger—the great "iron horse." Trains huffed and puffed their way onto the prairie, sending great clouds of ugly black coal dust and smoke into the clear air. It was the railroads, more than anything else, that brought swarms of white men to the Great Plains bent on slaughtering the buffalo herds unmercifully.

Why did these white men come from New York, Pennsylvania, Delaware, or the other states east of the Mississippi River? The answer is simple: for money.

In the early and mid-1800s, buffalo were killed by western pioneer settlers primarily for food and personal use, though a thriving trade in robes certainly existed, as noted earlier. It was also considered great sport to shoot buffalo from trains. The hides, however, had no extensive commercial value at this time. Unlike that of cattle, the buffalo's hide was too porous and spongy to make a widely marketable leather. The dramatic change that led to the demise of the buffalo, however, came in the early 1870s when an adequate process for tanning the hides was discovered. Suddenly, the plains were invaded by professional buffalo hunters. Thousands of buffalo were slaughtered daily; trains carried unbelievably high piles of hides back East for processing.

The simple, grazing buffalo paid little attention to the crack of the powerful guns used by the professional hide hunters. Dozens might die before a herd woke up to the fact that a hunter was somewhere nearby, reloading his long-range weapon as fast as he could. These men only wanted the hides, the big-money product. The meat was left untouched for the most part to rot or feed the wolves, ravens, and other scavengers. Soon the whole of the mighty plains was dotted with the putrefying remains of dead buffalo. The magnificent herds now became the victims of indiscriminate and wanton slaughter on a level never reached before or since in the hunting of an animal in American history.

The tribes that had built their way of life around the buffalo watched this slaughter in disbelief. Chief Kicking Bird of the Kiowas tried to explain the pain: "Just as it makes a white man's heart feel to have his money carried away, so it makes us feel to see others killing and stealing our buffaloes, which are our cattle given to us by the Great Father above to provide us meat to eat and means to get things to wear."[2]

Soulful pleas such as this went unheard, however. The slaughter continued at the hands of the commercial hunters while

Crow children watching white trappers

at the same time new settlers carved out a piece of America for themselves by taking land from the Indians. By the 1880s, only a few hundred buffalo lived where once millions had roamed as free as the wind, and the tribes that had walked the land were confined to United States government reservations.

"I love to roam over the prairies," noted the Kiowa chief Satanta when speaking with a sad heart of the prospects of reservation life. "There I feel free and happy, but when we settle down, we grow pale and die."[3]

"If you took me away from this land, it would be very hard for me," added Standing Bear of the Poncas. "I wish to die in this land. I wish to be an old man here."[4]

These Indians, however, did not have the military or political strength to hold onto their land, and so men such as Standing Bear, Satanta, and so many others could not "be an old man" on the land they once called home. Members of the Nez Percé tribe, like other Indians, were told by the United States government that they had to give up hunting and go live on a reservation. They

Train carrying hides while buffalo graze

A reservation

could learn how to farm just like the white man, the government reasoned. Some of the men who had hunted for so long expressed their feelings on farming with this native poem:

> You ask me to plow the gound
> Shall I take a knife and tear my mother's breast?
> Then when I die
> She will not take me to her bosom to sleep.
>
> You ask me to dig for stone.
> Shall I dig under her skin for bones?
> Then when I die
> I cannot enter her body to be born again.
>
> You ask me to cut grass and make hay,
> And sell it and be rich like the white man.
> But how dare I cut off my mother's hair
>
> It is a bad law and my people cannot obey it![5]

A LAST PRAYER

In 1881 a little-known Kiowa named Datekan, son of Woman's Heart and a medicine man, began to preach and foretell the return of the buffalo. He invited all the tribes from their reservation to a ceremony. He said the buffalo would return to earth from a hole covered by a flat rock inside a medicine lodge especially constructed to help him in his great effort. For ten days Datekan prayed, but the buffalo never returned. No medicine man or great spirit could make it happen, and Datekan, who had renamed himself Buffalo Bull Returns, died within the year.

The day of the buffalo and the
Moon of Falling Leaves has passed

Over the next few years, other Indians realized that the sun had set on their way of life forever. Never again would they have new buffalo robes to cut the chill of winter winds. The day of the buffalo had passed, the celebrated herds no longer darkened the horizon, the thunderous roar of the bulls no longer echoed across the prairie. Never again would the glorious glimmer of the Moon of Falling Leaves touch the tall and gracious grass of America's mighty Great Plains to signal the start of the heroic autumn buffalo hunt.

SOURCE NOTES

A COMMON ELEMENT

1. Katharine Berry Judson, *Myths and Legends of the Great Plains*, (Chicago, 1913), p. 53.

THE HORSE

1. Peter Nabokov, *Native American Testimony*, (New York, 1978), p. 50-53.

BUFFALO DANCE
1. Judson, *Myths and Legends of the Great Plains*, p. 51.

SCOUTS AND POLICE
1. Thomas Laurence Riggs, "Sunset to Sunset, a Lifetime with my Brothers, the Sioux," *South Dakota Department of History, Report and Historical Collections*, (Vol. XXIX, 1958), p. 228-243.
2. *Ibid.*
3. *Ibid.*
4. *Ibid.*

5. Karl N. Llewellyn and E. Adamson Hoebel, *The Cheyenne Way*, (Norman, Oklahoma, 1941), p. 102.
6. *Ibid.*

THE JUMP

1. David Dary, *The Buffalo Book*, (Chicago, 1974), p. 58.

WINTER

1. Peter Nabokov, *Two Leggings: The Making of a Crow Warrior*, (New York, 1967), p. 301.
2. *Ibid.*
3. *Ibid.*

FOOD, CLOTHING

1. Wayne Moquin, *Great Documents in American Indian History*, (New York, 1973), p. 62.
2. David J. Wishart, *The Fur Trade of the American West 1807-1840*, (Lincoln, Nebraska, 1979), p. 213.
3. Kai Erikson, "New Indian Wars," *Vanity Fair*, (March 1983), p. 97.
4. Wishart, *The Fur Trade of the American West 1807-1840*, p. 109.

THE HUNTING ENDS

1. Nabokov, *Native American Testimony*, p. 34.
2. Wayne Gard, *The Great Buffalo Hunt*, (New York, 1959), p. 155.
3. W. C. Vanderwerth, *Indian Oratory*, (Norman, Oklahoma, 1971), p. 180.
4. Dee Brown, *Bury My Heart at Wounded Knee*, (New York, 1970).
5. Dan Georgakas, *Red Shadows*, (New York, 1973), p. 121.

FOR FURTHER READING

Many of the books used to prepare this text are out of print or difficult to find. However, here are a few books and some recent articles about the buffalo which you can probably find at your local or school library.

Atwill, Lionel. "The Buffalo: An American Enigma." *Sports Afield*, December 1985, pp. 73-5, 126, 128.

Barsness, Larry. "The Bison in Art and History." *The American West*, March/April 1977, pp. 11-21.

Dary, David A. *The Buffalo Book*. Chicago: Swallow Press, 1974.

Haines, Francis. *The Buffalo*. New York: Crowell, 1970.

Haley, James L. "Prelude to War: The Slaughter of the Buffalo," *American Heritage*, February 1976, pp. 37-41, 82-89.

McHugh, Tom. *The Time of the Buffalo*. New York: Alfred Knopf, 1972.

Mitchell, John G. "Saved Just in Time, the Buffalo Graze Again on Our Plains," *Smithsonian*, May 1981, pp. 71-80.

Robbins, Jim. "After a 100-Year Hiatus, Bison Hunting Season Is Set to Begin." *New York Times*, November 11, 1985.

INDEX

ABOUT THE AUTHOR

Cary B. Ziter's literary repertoire ranges from articles for newspapers to scholarly journals to shoot-'em-up stories to comedy. He is currently an executive speechwriter for a major multinational corporation and lives with his family in upstate New York.

ABOUT THE ILLUSTRATOR

Gretchen Mayo holds a BS in Journalism from Marquette University in Wisconsin and a post-graduate teaching certificate from the University of Dayton (Ohio). She has also studied at the Milwaukee Institute of Art and Design. Ms. Mayo has been interested in and has sought out American Indian history, lore, and artifacts for many years. She and her husband and three children live in Whitefish Bay, Wisconsin.